故園畫憶

庚寅中秋 韓磐連題

《故园画忆系列》编委会

名誉主任：韩启德

主　　任：邵　鸿

委　　员：（按姓氏笔画为序）

万　捷	王秋桂	方李莉	叶培贵
刘魁立	况　晗	严绍璗	吴为山
范贻光	范　芳	孟　白	邵　鸿
岳庆平	郑培凯	唐晓峰	曹兵武

故园画忆系列
Memory of the Old
Home in Sketches

河北古建掠影
Hebei's Ancient Architecture

辛塞波 绘画 撰文
Sketches & Notes by Xin Saibo

学苑出版社
Academy Press

图书在版编目（CIP）数据

河北古建掠影：汉英对照 / 辛塞波绘、撰文. —北京：学苑出版社，2012.12
（故园画忆系列）
ISBN 978-7-5077-4186-5

Ⅰ. ①河… Ⅱ. ①辛… Ⅲ. ①古建筑－河北省－图集－汉、英
Ⅳ. ①K928.71-64

中国版本图书馆CIP数据核字(2012)第307058号

出 版 人：	孟 白
出版发行：	学苑出版社
社 　 址：	北京市丰台区南方庄2号院1号楼
邮政编码：	100079
网 　 址：	www.book001.com
电子信箱：	xueyuan@public.bta.net.cn
销售电话：	010-67601101（营销部）、67603091（总编室）
印 刷 厂：	三河市灵山红旗印刷厂
开本尺寸：	889×1194　1/24
印 　 张：	5.75
字 　 数：	100 千字
图 　 幅：	96幅
版 　 次：	2013年2月北京第1版
印 　 次：	2016年3月北京第2次印刷
定 　 价：	42.00元

目 录

自 序　　　　　　　　　辛塞波

承德
避暑山庄　　　　　　　　　　6
　澹泊敬诚殿　　　　　　　　6
　澹泊敬诚殿一角　　　　　　8
　延薰山馆　　　　　　　　　9
　水心榭　　　　　　　　　　10
　金山远眺　　　　　　　　　11
　金山阁楼　　　　　　　　　12
　天宇咸畅　　　　　　　　　13
　烟雨楼　　　　　　　　　　14
　烟雨楼远望　　　　　　　　15
　沧浪屿　　　　　　　　　　16
　文津阁　　　　　　　　　　17
　文津阁前廊　　　　　　　　18
　普陀宗乘之庙前的琉璃牌坊　19
须弥福寿之庙　　　　　　　　20
　山门　　　　　　　　　　　20
　琉璃牌坊　　　　　　　　　21
普宁寺　　　　　　　　　　　22
　大雄宝殿　　　　　　　　　22
　大乘阁　　　　　　　　　　24
　大乘阁寺内喇嘛塔（一）　　25
　大乘阁寺内喇嘛塔（二）　　26
普乐寺　　　　　　　　　　　28
　阁城远望　　　　　　　　　28
　万法归一殿　　　　　　　　30
　大红台小殿　　　　　　　　31
　吉祥法喜殿　　　　　　　　32
　旭光阁藻井及曼陀罗　　　　33

张家口
大境门　　　　　　　　　　　34
察哈尔总督署　　　　　　　　35
张家口堡子里　　　　　　　　36
　堡子里清真寺邦克楼　　　　36
　堡子里鼓楼　　　　　　　　38
　堡子里街景　　　　　　　　39
　堡子里门楼　　　　　　　　40
　堡子里影壁　　　　　　　　41
　堡子里四合院内景　　　　　42
　怡安街　　　　　　　　　　43
　清远楼　　　　　　　　　　44
　柏林寺塔　　　　　　　　　45
鸡鸣驿站　　　　　　　　　　46
　鸡鸣驿站城楼　　　　　　　46
　鸡鸣驿站文昌宫　　　　　　48
　鸡鸣驿站城楼一角　　　　　49
　鸡鸣驿站驿馆　　　　　　　50
　鸡鸣驿站影壁　　　　　　　51

鸡鸣驿站巷景	52
元中都遗址	53
开阳堡	54
南安寺塔	55
玉皇阁（一）	56
玉皇阁（二）	57
玉皇阁（三）	58
暖泉书院魁星楼	59
西古堡北门楼	60
西古堡北门楼一景	61
西古堡民居门楼（一）	62
西古堡民居门楼（二）	63

秦皇岛

源影塔	64
山海关城楼一角	65

唐山

清东陵	66
孝东陵方城明楼	68
景陵一角	69
裕陵	70
惠陵	72
唐山玉田净觉寺牌楼	73

保定

大旗杆	74
保定大悲阁	75
保定古莲池	76
碑刻长廊	77
水东楼	78
藻咏楼	79
直隶图书馆	80
保定光园正门	81
定州考棚	82
保定西大街	83
腰山王氏庄园	84
北岳庙德宁殿	85
北齐石柱	86
保定安国药王庙	87

石家庄

隆兴寺	88
摩尼殿	88
大悲阁	90
转轮藏阁	91
转轮藏	92
隆兴寺外	93
开元寺塔	94
正定广惠寺华塔	95
赵州桥	96
赵州桥栏板	97
陀罗尼经幢	98
赵州禅师舍利塔	99
井陉县天长镇城隍庙	100
城隍庙戏楼	101
福庆寺桥楼殿	102

衡水

宝云寺塔	103

邢台

邢台县英谈村	104
英谈村一景	105

邯郸

响堂山石窟	106
涉县娲皇阁	107

Contents

The Author's Preface   Xin Saibo

Chengde

Imperial Summer Resort	6
Danbo Jingcheng Hall	6
A View of Danbo Jingcheng Hall	8
Yanxun Hall	9
Shuixin Pavilion	10
Far-Reaching Jinshan Mountain	11
Pavilion on Jinshan Mountain	12
Tianyu Xianchang Hall	13
Yanyu Building	14
Look afar in Yanyu Building	15
Canglang Island	16
Wenjin Pavilion	17
Front Corridor of Wenjin Pavilion	18
Lazurite Memorial Archway in Front of Putuo Zongcheng Temple	19
Xumi Fushou Temple	20
Hill Gate	20
Lazurite Memorial Archway	21
Puning Temple	22
Daxiong Shrine Hall	22
Dacheng Pavilion	24
Lama Tower in Dacheng Pavilion (1)	25
Lama Tower in Dacheng Pavilion (2)	26
Pule Temple	28
Looking afar from Ducheng	28
Wanfa Guiyi Hall	30
Small Hall on Dahong Platform	31
Jixiang Faxi Hall	32
Ceiling and Mandala of Xuguang Pavilion	33

Zhangjiakou

Dajing Gate	34
Chaha'er Governor's Office	35
Zhangjiakou Buzili	36
Buzili Masjid Mi'dhanah	36
Buzili Bell Tower	38
Buzili Streets	39
Buzili Gatehouse	40
Buzili Screen Wall	41
View within a Buzili Courtyard House	42
Yi'an Street	43
Qingyuan Building	44
Bolin Temple Pagoda	45
Jiming Post Station	46
Jiming Post Station Gate Tower	46
Wenchang Temple in Jiming Post Station	48
View of Jiming Post Station Gate Tower	49
Inn in Jiming Post Station	50
Screen Wall of Jiming Post Station	51
Lane in Jiming Post Station	52

Yuanzhong City Relic	53
Kaiyang Fort	54
Nan'an Temple Pagoda	55
Jade Emperor's Palace (1)	56
Jade Emperor's Palace (2)	57
Jade Emperor's Palace (3)	58
Kuixing Building in Nuanquan Academy	59
North Gatehouse of Xigubu	60
View of North Gatehouse, Xigubu	61
Residential Gatehouse of Xigubu (1)	62
Residential Gatehouse of Xigubu (2)	63

Qinhuangdao

Yuanying Pagoda	64
View of Shanhai Pass City Tower	65

Tangshan

Qingdong Mausoleum	66
Xiaodong Mausoleum Fangcheng Ming Building	68
View of Jingling Mausoleum	69
Yuling Mausoleum	70
Huiling Mausoleum	72
Tangshan Yutian Jingjue Temple Archway	73

Baoding

Great Flagpole	74
Baoding Dabei Pavilion	75
Baoding Ancient Lotus Pond	76
Tablet Gallery	77
Shuidong Building	78
Zaoyong Building	79
Zhili Library	80
Gate of Baoding Guangyuan Garden	81
Dingzhou Examination Hall	82
Baoding Xida Street	83
Wang's Manor in Yaoshan	84
Beiyue Temple Dening Hall	85
Beiqi Stone Column	86
Baoding An'guo Yaowang Temple	87

Shijiazhuang

Longxing Temple	88
Moni Hall	88
Dabei Pavilion	90
Zhuanlun Collection Pavilion	91
Zhuanlun Repository	92
Longxing Temple Setting	93
Kaiyuan Temple Pagoda	94
Zhengding Huata Pagoda of Guanghui Temple	95
Zhaozhou Bridge	96
Stone Fascia Panels of Zhaozhou Bridge	97
Dharani Sutra Pillar	98
Stupa of Buddhist Monk Zhaozhou	99
Town God Temple of Tianchang, Jingxing County	100
Opera Stage of Town God Temple	101
Bridge House Palace of Fuqing Temple	102

Hengshui

Baoyun Temple Pagoda	103

Xingtai

Yingtan Village, Xingtai County	104
View of Yingtan Village	105

Handan

Xiangtangshan Grottoes	106
Nüwa Goddess Pavilion, She County	107

自 序

在人们的印象中，中国古代建筑以河南、山西、陕西三省的名气最大，河北似乎逊色了一些。河北既无北京的大气，又无天津的洋气，也不比河南、山西的久远，人们对北方古代建筑的目光很少停留在河北地区。但是单以拥有全国级重点文物保护单位的数量来算，在国务院公布的242处第一、二批全国重点文物保护单位名单中，河北省占了24处，与陕西并列第一。河北位于北京、天津两市的外围，自古即是京畿要地。作为清代皇室的勤政、郊游场所，河北省东北部的承德是我国最早命名的历史文化名城之一，这里有清代最大的皇家园林避暑山庄，中国最大的皇家寺庙群——"外八庙"。此外，河北著名的古代建筑还有涉县娲皇宫、邯郸响堂山石窟、保定直隶总督署和古莲池、易县清西陵、唐山清东陵、赵县赵州桥、正定隆兴寺等。不仅有如此众多的历史古迹，河北还不乏风景秀丽的自然景观，山、水、林各种景致相映相成，为燕赵大地增添了不少色彩。故园如何从对个人记忆和经验的回溯转化为对河北悠久历史的回顾，是我一直萦绕于心的一个愿望。

考察河北古迹的计划不断发自心底地向我挑战，我决定通过自己的建筑语言——"画忆"来做出回答，最终的结果是它的确开阔了我的眼界。它超越了时间与现在的我进行对话，当我真正地面对历史遗存时，才觉得历史原来是如此真切和感人。面对鲜活的河北古建筑，我不禁有通过自己手中的笔和纸把它们画下来的愿望和渴求。我不想把历史当作怀旧情结，而是把它作为充满活力的过去。一座座历史建筑被图像化的过程展示出它们曾经有过的设计和施工方式、历史景观演绎和变迁的过程；牵连出的一系列历史事件耐人寻味地叙述着历史的跌宕起伏，让我沉醉其中……

相对于钢筋混凝土构筑的现代建筑，传统建筑常能令人回想起那些拥有精湛技艺与个性特征的时代，而这些技艺与个性特征在现代工业化的建造手段与建造系统中都已消失殆尽。所以，人们对那些手工生产的、经历了历史沧桑的、由自然材料建造的建筑有一种本能的认同感，不仅希望能对其进行保护，还希望能修复与挖掘其更深层次的文化价值。

我的旅程从张家口到承德，再从那儿坐火车经由北京到达保定、沧州、正定、邯郸……两年的列车旅程伴随着山脉的起伏和平原的辽阔，让我心旷神怡。实地考察河北省古代建筑，将建筑绘画与历史文献内容综合，极大地促使我理解历史建筑的价值内涵，提高了我的美学修养。通过对河北古建筑的绘画，我不仅了解和掌握了这些古代建筑的基本特征和建筑风格，而且深入理解了中国建筑精神的起源和历史场景对今日城市生活的影响，它让我意识到我们个人的前途和所生活城市的未来应该与这些古老的建筑有所联系，眼下最重要的是我们应该具有怎样的意识、采取什么样的办法来竭尽全力地保护它们。城市本质上是一个新陈代谢的动态有机体，如何保护燕赵大地上弥足珍贵的古建筑遗产，关键问题是如何把握城市文化传承、历史延续与社会经济发展的关系。

2012年6月于河北坝上

The Author's Preface

It's generally believed that Henan, Shanxi and Shaanxi are the three provinces with the most renowned ancient architecture in China, but Hebei architecture is somewhat less impressive being neither as magnificent as Beijing, as exotic as Tianjin, nor as ancient as Henan and Shanxi. It attracts little attention from those interested in ancient architecture in northern China. However, in terms of the quantity of national key cultural relic protection sites, Hebei has 24 national key cultural relic protected sites listed in first and second group published by the State Council, which has a total of 242 protected sites. Hebei ranks first along with Shaanxi. Located in the vicinity of Beijing and Tianjin, Hebei was an important strategic area of the capital city since ancient times. As the locale for political practice and outings of the Qing royal family, Chengde, in northeast Hebei, is one of the earliest historical, cultural cities of China. It has the largest imperial summer resort of the Qing Dynasty and the largest imperial temple in China – *Wai Ba Miao* (外八庙), "External Eight Temples". The famous ancient architecture in Hebei also includes Xianwa Imperial Palace, Handan Xiangtang Mountain stone cave, Baoding Governor's Office of Zhili (former name of He Bei) Province, an ancient lotus pond, Qingxi Mausoleum in Yixian County, Qingdong Mausoleum in Tangshan, Zhaozhou Bridge in Zhaoxian County, Zhengding Longxing Temple and so on. In addition to numerous historical ancient relics, Hebei has enchanting mountain, river and forest natural scenery adding wonder to this ancient area. Relating the personal memories and experiences of my Old Home to a review of the long history of Hebei has long been a wish lingering in my heart.

How to investigate Hebei's ancient relics has long challenged me, but, spontaneously. I decided to use my own architectural language "sketching from memory", and I have broadened my outlook as a consequence. This is a dialogue between the "present me" and the "past me". When I actually stand in front of a historical relic, I find its history vivid and touching. The desire to record the ancient architecture with pen and paper was aroused when standing before the vivid ancient architecture of Hebei. History is a vigorous "bygone" rather than just nostalgia. The design, construction, landscape evolution, and the development of the historical architecture in these paintings have emotionally revealed to me the historical events that tell the vicissitudes of these sites. I am really obsessed by it all.

Compared to the reinforced concrete of modern buildings, traditional architecture reminds us more of the excellent skills and specific eras, which have vanished due to modern industrialized construction methods and architectural designs. Therefore, people recognize in these manually-built structures of natural materials that have experienced great changes. They desire to protect and to reconstruct so as to reveal its profound cultural value.

My trip took me from Zhangjiakou to Chengde, Beijing, Baoding, Cangzhou, Zhengding, Handan... – this two-year journey by train refreshed my memory of the undulating ridges and the vast plain. Investigating the ancient architecture of Hebei, studying the historical literature, and enjoying the on-site painting experience have greatly helped me understand the value of ancient architecture and enhanced my aesthetic achievement. During the painting of ancient structures in Hebei, I better understood and mastered the basic features, the style of this ancient architectures and the origin of Chinese architectural philosophy, as well as realized the affection for historical scenes in our modern urban lives. I became aware that our personal prospects and the future of the cities in which we live are connected to this ancient architecture. Now, most important is how to protect it with our full awareness. A city is a dynamic organic entity that evolves over time, but how do we protect the rare, ancient architecture in Hebei? The key lies in understanding the relationships among urban cultural heritage, historical extension, and social and economic development.

Xin Saibo
Hebei Bashang Prairie
Jun. 2012

避暑山庄

又名承德离宫或热河行宫，位于承德市中心。建造于18世纪初，由皇帝宫室、皇家园林和宏伟壮观的寺庙群组成。承德避暑山庄是世界文化遗产。

Imperial Summer Resort

Location: Chengde

Known as Chengde or Rehe Palace, it is located in the center of Chengde. It was built at the beginning of the 18th century and composed of the imperial palace and gardens and beautiful temples.
The Resort has been listed as a World Cultural Heritage.

澹泊敬诚殿

澹泊敬诚殿位于避暑山庄南面的行宫部分。此殿是举行重大典礼、接待外使政要的地方。因用楠木建造，俗称楠木殿。康熙五十年（1711）初建，乾隆十九年（1754）改建。大殿面积612平方米。殿式为卷棚歇山顶，青砖、灰瓦、梁柱、隔扇、天花均为本色楠木。周廊及室内地面由天然紫豆瓣大理石铺砌。

Danbo Jingcheng Hall

Location: Imperial Summer Resort

Located in the south of the Imperial Summer Resort, Danbo Jingcheng Hall is for significant ceremonies and receptions of foreign envoys and officers. It is known as Nanmu Hall because it's built of Nanmu. It was initially built in 1711 and rebuilt in 1754.

2009年5月

澹泊敬诚殿一角

康熙借用"非淡泊无以明志,非宁静无以致远"这种观念指导自己的行为,同时教育子孙要"以静修身、以简养德",说的是政治上要高瞻远瞩,生活上要简朴淡泊。澹泊敬诚殿妙就妙在其丰厚的文化内涵和深邃的帝王治世思想。

A View of Danbo Jingcheng Hall

Location: Imperial Summer Resort

Emperor Kangxi told his descendants to "cultivate the soul in tranquility and cultivate morality with simplicity", which refers to seeing far and wide in politics but living simply with indifference to fame and wealth. The Danbo Jingcheng Hall has profound cultural connotations and subtle ideas of the emperor's governance.

2012年1月

延薰山馆

避暑山庄内有一组四合院式建筑，正殿名为"延薰山馆"。面阔七间，前带五楹抱厦，单檐歇山卷棚顶。康熙帝早期在此亲政。取"延薰"二字暗示皇帝廉洁清明、怀柔远人、施政仁厚。院内古松挺拔、青草茸茸，充满诗情画意。

Yanxun Hall

Location: Imperial Summer Resort

In this courtyard house in Imperial Summer Resort, the front hall "Yanxun Hall" is where Emperor Kangxi handled political affairs in earlier days. "Yanxun" implies incorruptibility and the conciliatory and benevolent policies of the Qing Emperor.

2010年5月

水心榭

水心榭位于避暑山庄跨湖石桥之上，中间是重檐歇山卷棚顶的建筑，两端为重檐攒尖顶的建筑。三间建筑物比例匀称，组织紧密，其下承以石梁。影子倒入湖中，与四周山光相映衬，秀丽如画。康熙帝亲笔题名"水心榭"。

Shuixin Pavilion

Location: Imperial Summer Resort

Shuixin Pavilion is located on the bridge spanning over the lake in the Imperial Summer Resort. In the middle is a building with double-eave gable and parabolic roof; on the two sides are double-eave roof buildings. Decorated archways with four pillars have been built on two ends of the Pavilion. Emperor Kangxi inscribed "Shuixin Pavilion" for it.

2010年11月

金山远眺

在避暑山庄跨湖东岸附近，有一小岛，谓之金山。金山之上有阁楼及殿五间，外有过山曲廊，回环曲折，高低参差，形如半月环抱。

康熙皇帝南巡时，多次登江苏镇江金山游览，醉心于江流天际的壮丽景色，后在山庄水面开阔的澄湖东部修筑了金山岛。避暑山庄的金山与镇江的金山相比，规模虽小，但景物环境相似。

Far-Reaching Jinshan Mountain

Location: Imperial Summer Resort

Emperor Kangxi climbed Jinshan Mountain several times during his southward trips because he was so infatuated with the beautiful landscape. Later, he built Jinshan Island in the east of vast Chenghu Lake. Although Jinshan Mountain in the Imperial Summer Resort is smaller than the mountains in Zhenjiang, it resembles the environment and landscape.

2012年2月

2012年1月

金山阁楼

金山有阁,三层八角,称"皇穹永佑",殿下巨石如云。

Pavilion on Jinshan Mountain

Location: Imperial Summer Resort

The pavilion on Jinshan Mountain with three storeys and eight corners is known as "Blessed by Imperial Power". Under the pavilion are countless huge stones.

> 天宇咸畅

此殿约建于1703年至1708年，位于金山峰顶的平台上，是一座面阔三楹、进深两间、四周围廊的面南大殿，康熙题为"天宇咸畅"。在此俯瞰湖山洲岛、鸟飞鱼跃，更觉风景壮丽。

Tianyu Xianchang Hall

Location: Imperial Summer Resort

Located on the plateau of the peak of Jinshan Mountain, the hall was built between 1703 and 1708. It is a south facing hall with three horizontal rooms, two vertical rooms and surrounding corridor. Emperor Kangxi inscribed "Tianyu Xianchang" for it.

2008年5月

烟雨楼

从如意洲越曲桥登岛，南有门殿三间。穿过门殿，迎面为二层楼一座，卷棚歇山布瓦顶，上下围廊以苏画装饰。前檐高悬乾隆皇帝题写的云龙金匾"烟雨楼"，楹联为："百尺起空蒙碧涵莲岛，八窗临渺弥澄印鸳湖。"

Yanyu Building

Location: Imperial Summer Resort

From Yuequ Bridge to reach on Ruyi Islet, three gates can be seen in the south. Walking through the gates, visitors find a two-storey building with gable and parabolic tiled roof, upper and lower fence and decoration of Suzhou painting. On the front eave hangs a dragon gold tablet with "Yanyu Building", inscribed by Emperor Kangxi.

2010年10月

【烟雨楼远望】

乾隆皇帝南巡时，在嘉兴南湖鸳鸯岛上，见五代吴越文陵王钱元璙所建烟雨楼布局灵活、造型秀丽，回京后遂按烟雨楼意境，在山庄仿建。烟雨楼北、西廊外，湖中起台，置汉白玉望柱。

Look afar in Yanyu Building

Location: Imperial Summer Resort

Emperor Qianlong visited the Yanyu Building of Emperor Wenling of Wuyue on Yuanyang Island in South Lake in Jiaxing during his trip to the south. He built a similar Yanyu Building in the resort according to the original's layout and enchanting style.

2010年10月

沧浪屿

　　沧浪屿始建于康熙年间，在如意洲东北角上西岭晨霞阁后面。沿石阶小路向东有三开间的房屋一所，窗户向北临池，房后檐悬挂康熙手书匾额"沧浪屿"。自南踏石阶入垂花门，满院山石嶙峋，经弯曲的小径，有室三间，系康熙读书之所。

Canglang Island

Location: Imperial Summer Resort

Canglang Island was initially built during the reign of Qing Emperor Kangxi. It is behind the Chenxia Pavilion on the West Ridge northeast of Ruyi Islet.

2010年5月

【文津阁】

　　文津阁位于万树园以西的山脚下,建于乾隆三十九年(1774),是仿浙江宁波天一阁的建筑布局和样式所建。无论是整体布局、体量尺寸、建筑用材和施工方法,还是书架款式,都与天一阁相仿。文津阁外观两层,实际是三层,中间一层是阳光不能直射的藏书库。

Wenjin Pavilion

Location: Imperial Summer Resort

Located at the western edge of Wanshu Garden, Wenjin Pavilion was built in 1774 imitating the layout pattern of Tianyi Pavilion in Ningbo, Zhejiang.

2009年12月

2009年12月

文津阁前廊

文津阁曾珍藏《古今图书集成》、《四库全书》各一部。文津阁和北京紫禁城内的文渊阁、圆明园的文源阁、沈阳故宫的文溯阁合称内廷四库（或北方四阁），是贮藏《四库全书》的地方。

Front Corridor of Wenjin Pavilion

Location: Imperial Summer Resort

Wenjin Pavilion has housed *A Collection of Ancient and Modern Albums and Books* and *The Complete Collection in Four Treasuries*.

普陀宗乘之庙前的琉璃牌坊

　　普陀宗乘之庙位于避暑山庄之北狮子沟的北山坡上,是承德"外八庙"之一。"普陀宗乘"是藏语"布达拉"的意思,因此,普陀宗乘之庙又称小布达拉宫。普陀宗乘之庙南部有一座高大精美的汉式琉璃牌坊,中楼前额"普门应现",意观音显现普度众生之门,后额"莲界庄严",意为观音道场。牌坊正南台阶两侧立有雄武石狮一对,增加了牌坊的气势。

Lazurite Memorial Archway in Front of Putuo Zongcheng Temple

Location: Chengde

Located on the north slope of Lion Ditch north of the Imperial Summer Resort, Putuo Zongcheng Temple is one of the "External Eight Temples" of Chengde. To the south of Putuo Zongcheng Temple there is a tall, delicate Han-style lazurite memorial archway. The front tablet in the middle – "Pumen Yingxian" means the gate where Guanyin appears and helps the people. "Lianjie Zhuangyan" on the back of the tablet refers to the place where Guanyin holds rites.

2010年6月

2009年12月

须弥福寿之庙

　　须弥福寿之庙是承德"外八庙"之一，位于避暑山庄北面狮子沟南坡，自山脚顺山势向上延伸，气势雄伟。整个庙宇自南而北有山门、碑亭、琉璃牌坊、大红台、金贺堂、万德宗源殿、琉璃万寿塔等主要建筑，沿一条较明显的中轴线采取左右基本对称的布局排列。

Xumi Fushou Temple
Location: Chengde

Xumi Fushou Temple is one of the "External Eight Temples" of Chengde. Located on the south slope of Lion Ditch in the north of the Imperial Summer Resort, it is a lovely temple extending from the mountain's foot to its peak.

山门

　　山门南向，有三个拱门，上建门楼，和普陀宗乘之庙的山门略同，周围以墙壁围绕。

Hill Gate
Location: Xumi Fushou Temple

Hill Gate faces south. There are three arches with gatehouses atop. Enclosed by walls, it is similar to the Hill Gate of Putuo Zongcheng Temple.

琉璃牌坊

　　须弥福寿之庙碑亭以北，有一座三间四柱七楼式琉璃牌坊。上有云龙等图案组成的饰件，五光十色，光彩夺目。牌坊翼角翘起，斗拱层叠。整座牌坊用黄绿琉璃和青砖构成，体现出皇家气派。牌楼前两侧置石象一对，雕刻精美，寓意"万象更新"。

Lazurite Memorial Archway
Location: Xumi Fushou Temple
To the north of the stele pavilion of Xumi Fushou Temple is a three-room four-pillar seven-storey lazurite memorial archway built with yellow and green lazurite and blue bricks, reflecting the imperial style.

2010年6月

普宁寺

普宁寺位于避暑山庄北部武烈河河畔，建成于乾隆二十年（1755），是"外八庙"宗教活动的中心。普宁寺的修建和取名都表明皇帝希望天下永远太平统一、人民安居乐业。

Puning Temple

Location: Chengde

Located by the bank of Wulie River, north of the Imperial Summer Resort, Puning Temple was built in 1755. It is the center of religious activities of the "External Eight Temples". The construction and name of Puning Temple reflects the hope of the Qing Emperor to achieve eternal harmony and peace.

大雄宝殿

大雄宝殿是普宁寺的主体建筑，建在1.4米高的石砌须弥台基之上。殿前月台环绕着雕刻精美的石栏杆，台阶中央铺有石雕艺术精品"云龙石陛"，四角有叫"螭"的龙头。此殿为双层歇山式，称为"九脊十龙"殿。

Daxiong Shrine Hall

Location: Puning Temple

Daxiong Shrine Hall is the main building of Puning Temple. It was built on a 1.4m stone foundation.

2010年7月

> 大乘阁

　　大乘阁是普宁寺的后部中心，是一座高大的木结构楼阁式建筑，最顶层四角安四个攒尖方顶，上具宝顶。

Dacheng Pavilion

Location: Puning Temple

Dacheng Pavilion is the rear center of Puning Temple. It is a tall wooden pavilion-style building. The top floor has four separate traditional tipped roofs.

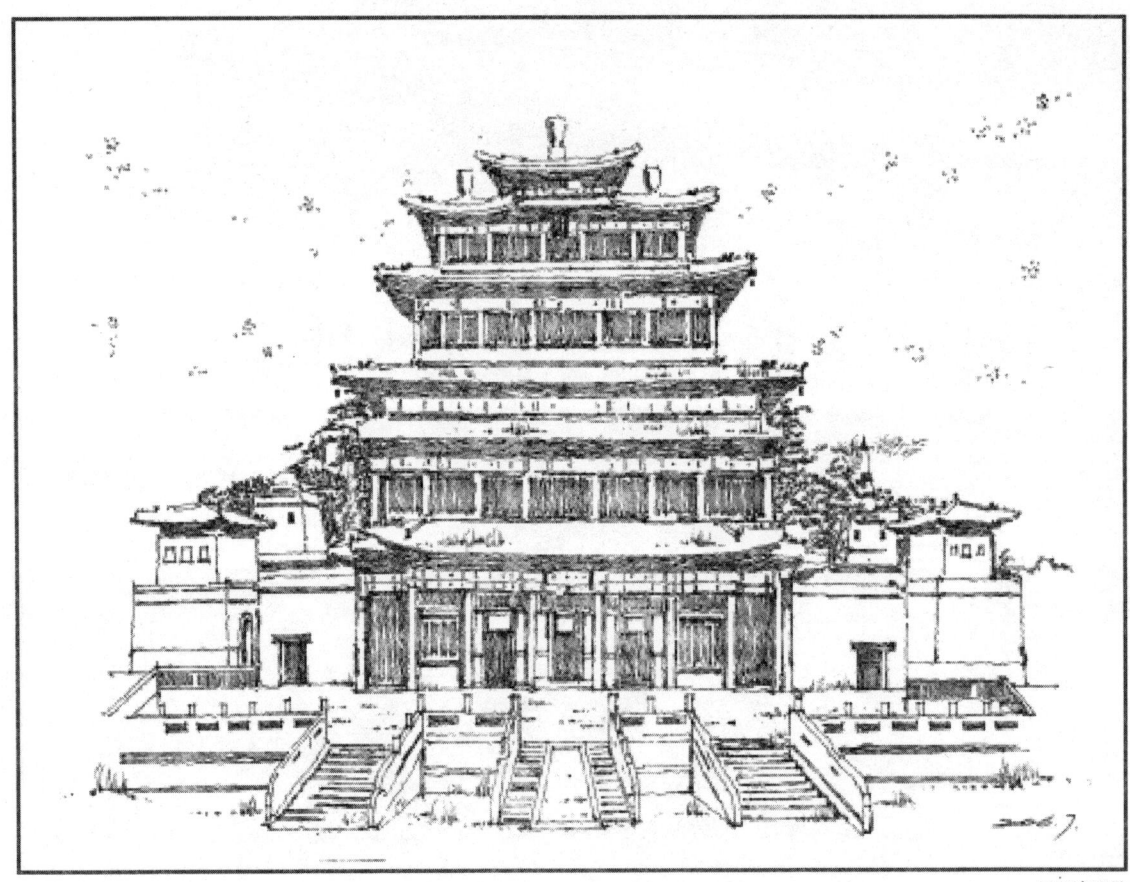

2006年7月

大乘阁寺内喇嘛塔（一）

　　大乘阁的四角内侧耸立着四座颜色不同、造型各异的喇嘛塔。塔顶有金属宝盖和日月宝珠火焰。画面为其中一座喇嘛塔。

Lama Tower in Dacheng Pavilion (1)

Location: Puning Temple

On each of the four corners of Dacheng Pavilion there is a Lama tower of different colors and styles. Atop each tower is a metal flame-shape ball. This drawing shows one of the towers.

2010年6月

【大乘阁寺内喇嘛塔（二）】

　　喇嘛塔依山就势，布局巧妙灵活，是一组精美的藏式风格寺庙建筑。

Lama Tower in Dacheng Pavilion (2)
Location: Puning Temple
This Tibetan Lama tower of exquisite, distinct design is on the hillside.

2008年6月

普乐寺

普乐寺位于避暑山庄以东武烈河东岸，建于乾隆三十一年（1766），寺门西向。全寺建筑为汉藏结合式，西部依照汉族寺庙样式由山门、天王殿、钟鼓楼、配殿、正殿组成，东部为藏式建筑。

Pule Temple

Location: Chengde

Located on the east bank of Wulie River at the east of the Imperial Summer Resort, Pule Temple was built in 1766 with a west facing gate. The architecture has both Han and Tibetan styles.

阇城远望

阇城是藏传佛教密宗修炼、观摩、传授秘法之道场。从平面上看，阇城分为内外三重，台顶四周环布琉璃喇嘛塔八座，有五种不同的颜色，甚是漂亮。

Looking afar from Ducheng

Location: Pule Temple

Ducheng of Pule Temple is where Buddhists practice, observe and teach doctrines. Ducheng has three layers. On top are eight lazurite Lama towers of five different colors, creating an appealing scene.

2010年7月

> 万法归一殿

　　坐落在条石须弥座上的大殿便是普乐寺的主殿——万法归一殿。它位于群楼中心,既显示出了藏传佛教的崇高地位,也隐含了皇权的中心地位。整个大殿被誉为金殿,奢华精美的建筑风格让人叹为观止。

Wanfa Guiyi Hall
Location: Pule Temple
Wanfa Guiyi Hall is the main hall of Pule Temple. It is located at the center of all buildings, revealing the noble status of Tibetan Buddhism and the core position of imperial power. The hall is honored as Gold Hall for its astonishing luxurious, exquisite architectural style.

2010年6月

> 大红台小殿

  大红台顶部平坦，四角各建有庑殿顶式小殿一座，形态舒展，造型优美，琉璃瓦顶，脊上吻兽（南面两殿为孔雀，北面两殿为鹿）。各殿皆面阔三间，进深三间，内供金刚佛像。

Small Hall on Dahong Platform

Location: Pule Temple

Dahong Platform has a small hip-roofed hall on each corner. They are beautiful expansively laid out with lazurite tile roof with beasts on the ridges (peacock in south two halls and deer in north two halls).

2010年6月

2009年6月

吉祥法喜殿

　　班禅居住的吉祥法喜殿位于大红台的右边，表示小于皇权，但为了尊敬班禅，吉祥法喜殿的地势又高于皇帝休息的场所"御座楼"。

Jixiang Faxi Hall

Location: Pule Temple

Jixiang Faxi Hall, the living quarters of the Banchan Lama, is located at the right of Dahong Platform, implying his subordinate status to imperial power. However, in order to pay respect to the Banchan Lama, Jixiang Faxi Hall is higher than "Yuzuo Building" where emperors rested.

旭光阁藻井及曼陀罗

　　普乐寺旭光阁大殿做圆形藻井，向上凸达3米，共分六圈，顶部有二龙戏珠。藻井采用层层收缩的三层重翘重昂九踩斗拱手法，雕工精细，具有极高的艺术价值。阁内中央，在圆形的石造须弥座之上，建有一立体的曼陀罗。曼陀罗是宗教仪式中的圆圈，在佛教中代表了宣传平等的宗教思想。

Ceiling and Mandala of Xuguang Pavilion

Location: Pule Temple

Xuguang Pavilion has a round, 3m deep coved ceiling. There are six circles and caving of two dragons playing ball on the top. The ceiling has three-layer overlapped exquisitely carved wood brackets. They are of greet artistic value. In the center of the pavilion on the round stone seat is a three dimensional Mandala.

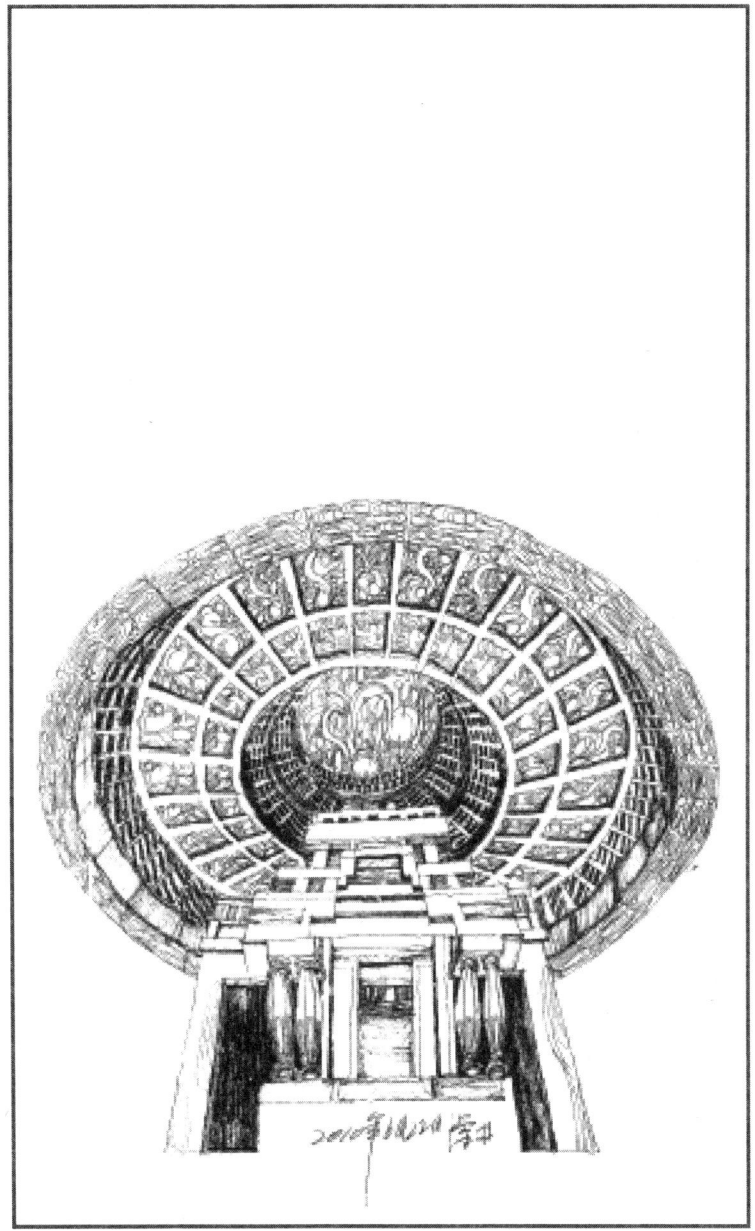

2010年6月

大境门

张家口在清代是北方十分重要的商业都市,被称为"陆路商埠"。大境门位于张家口市区北部,处于东、西太平山之间,是万里长城的一个关隘,历史上是扼守京都的北大门。大境门是一座条石基础的砖砌拱门,门墙高12米,底长13米,宽9米,有木质铁皮大门两扇。顶部为一平台,长12米,宽7.5米,外有1.7米高的垛口,内有0.8米高的女儿墙,东部有台阶可上。门楣上有时任察哈尔都统高维岳于1927年所题的四个颜体大字"大好河山",每字足有一米见方,笔力苍劲。

Dajing Gate

Location: Zhangjiakou

Zhangjiakou was a very important northern commercial city during the Qing Dynasty, well known as a "commercial land port". Dajing Gate is located at the north of Zhangjiakou between East Taiping Mountain and West Taiping Mountain. It is the north gate in the Great Wall guarding the capital in time gone by.

2010年6月

察哈尔总督署

察哈尔总督署位于张家口市上堡明德北街三角地，是张家口市唯一保存较为完整的清代官衙建筑。衙署始建于清乾隆二十七年（1762），坐北朝南，现存四进院落，布局完好。察哈尔总督署是河北省重点文物保护单位。

Chaha'er Governor's Office
Location: Zhangjiakou

Chaha'er Governor's Office, located in a triangle block of Mingde North Street, Shangbu, is the only well-preserved official Qing building in Zhangjiakou. The office was built in 1762 with a south-facing gate. Four courtyards have been preserved.

2002年11月

张家口堡子里

堡子里是张家口堡的俗称。张家口堡是张家口市区最早的城堡，张家口市区的"原点"与"根"。据史籍记载，堡子里建于明宣德年间（1426~1435），是全国大中城市中保存最为完整的明清建筑城堡之一，堪称北方民居博物馆。堡子里是河北省重点文物保护单位。

Zhangjiakou Buzili

Location: Zhangjiakou

Buzili is the proverb of Zhangjiakoubu. Zhangjiakoubu is the earliest castle built within the town. According to historical records, Buzili was built during the reign of Ming Emperor Xuande (1426-1435). It is one of the most well preserved Ming/Qing castles built in medium or large cities nationwide.

堡子里清真寺邦克楼

堡子里清真寺坐落于堡子里南城墙外的西关街底，建于康熙八年（1669），雍正、乾隆年间曾多次重修和扩建，是一座穆斯林文化与中国传统的建筑形式完美结合的建筑。清真寺南侧跨院内有一座重檐六角攒尖亭（邦克楼），与大殿攒尖顶相呼应。

Buzili Masjid Mi'dhanah

Location: Zhangjiakou Buzili

Located below West Pass outside the south city wall of Buzili, the Buzili Masjid is a perfect combination of Muslim and traditional Chinese architecture. Built in 1669, it has a double-eave six-corner tip roof pavilion (Mi'dhanah) in the south courtyard of Masjid; it echoes the tip roof of the hall.

2007年11月

| 堡子里鼓楼 |

　　鼓楼又称文昌阁，始建于明万历四十七年（1619），坐落于张家口市中心的堡子里中心，有四条主要街道在它的基座下面交汇。楼阁由墩台和楼阁两部分组成，底层四门通衢。鼓楼外观比例适宜，鼓楼由于其高大的体量及中心位置，成为该地区的中心和标志。

Buzili Bell Tower
Location: Zhangjiakou Buzili

Buzili Bell Tower, also known as Wenchang Pavilion, was built in 1619 in Buzili Center in Zhangjiakou. Four main streets met at its base. The Drum Tower is the center and landmark of this region.

2010年8月

{ 堡子里街景 }

穿行于堡子里胡同之间，能感受到浓郁的生活气息。道路两侧的民居虽略显破旧，甚至有墙皮脱落，但是与当地人的生活水乳交融。

Buzili Streets

Location: Zhangjiakou Buzili

A bustling atmosphere fills the Hutongs across Buzili. Although residential buildings along two sides of the roads are old and shabby with some walls in disrepair, they are in harmony with local life.

2010年6月

堡子里门楼

门楼是住宅外观塑造的重中之重，对于丰富街区景观起到了非常重要的作用。堡子里的门楼各有特色，形成了街巷里一个个小的焦点，活跃了街景。

Buzili Gatehouse

Location: Zhangjiakou Buzili

The gatehouse is a very significant part of the exterior appearance of a house and plays an important role in enriching the streetscape. Gatehouses in Buzili have varied features, forming tiny foci of the lanes and streets and invigorate the streetscape.

2007年2月

堡子里影壁

　　堡子里街区的墙面变化丰富，在正房的山墙上常刻有精致的砖雕，做工精美。这座四合院内影壁正中央写有"燕禧"二字，造型漂亮。

Buzili Screen Wall

Location: Zhangjiakou Buzili

Walls in Buzili streets have rich designs. Usually the gabled walls are engraved with exquisite brick carvings. In the screen wall of this courtyard house, there are two beautifully written words "Yan Xi".

2007年2月

| 堡子里四合院内景 |

　　物换星移，沧桑变幻，堡子里依然保持着明清时代的建筑风貌。这里的古建筑原汁原味，这些主要由晋商建筑的民居，与山西平遥的古民居一样，使人惊奇、使人赞叹。

View within a Buzili Courtyard House

Location: Zhangjiakou Buzili

Though time flies and the world changes, Buzili maintains the architectural style of Ming and Qing dynasties.

2007年5月

> 怡安街

　　张家口怡安街因京张铁路而生，始建于清光绪三十二年（1906），因由"怡安产业公司"修建而得名。繁盛时的怡安街店铺众多，真可谓是商贾云集、买卖兴旺，是京、冀、晋等周边地区闻名遐迩的一条商业街。如今怡安街繁华不再，步履蹒跚，饱经风霜。

Yi'an Street

Location: Zhangjiakou

This street got its name from the building Constructed in 1906 by the "Yi'an Industrial Company". In that prosperous era, there were numerous shops and stores in Yi'an Street, which was the famous business street for neighboring regions in Beijing, Hebei and Shanxi. Yi'an Street is no longer busy, but merely a run down weather-beaten street.

2002年10月

> 清远楼

清远楼位于张家口市宣化区镇朔楼正北,又名钟楼,始建于明成化十八年(1482)。楼建在高8米的十字券洞上,楼下东南西北各通安定、昌平、大新、广灵四座城门。楼外观三层,内实两层,通高25米,楼阁高17米,前后明间出抱厦,四周有游廊。清远楼是全国重点文物保护单位。

Qingyuan Building

Location: Zhangjiakou

Built in 1482, Qingyuan Building, also known as Bell Tower, is located in the north of the Zhenshuo building, Xuanhua District, Zhangjiakou. It was built on a terrace 8m high. From here, roads lead to the four city gates: Anding, Changping, Daxin and Guangling.

2008年7月

柏林寺塔

柏林寺位于宣化城南35公里的柏林寺村西小环山北坡上，北魏时修建。柏林寺佛塔高12米，为八角形五层实心石塔，第一至第四层是在岩石上凿刻而成，第五层用八块石料雕刻后安装，塔顶和塔刹也为石料雕刻后装配而成。柏林寺塔是河北省重点文物保护单位。

Bolin Temple Pagoda

Location: Zhangjiakou

Built in North Wei Dynasty(386-557), Bolin Temple is located on the north slope of Xixiaohuan Hill of Bolin Temple Village 35 km from Xuanhua South. Buddha Pagoda of Bolin Temple is a 12m high five-storey octagonal solid stone pagoda. F/1-F/4 was directly chiseled out of the rock while F/5 was constructed with eight carved stones.

2006年11月

鸡鸣驿站

鸡鸣驿站位于怀来县洋河北岸的鸡鸣山下，是目前国内保存最好、规模最大、最富有特色的邮驿建筑群，具有重要的历史、艺术价值，被称为邮政考古、机要考古的一座"活化石"。

Jiming Post Station

Location: Huailai County, Zhangjiakou

Jiming Post Station, located at the foot of Jiming Mountain on the north bank of the Yanghe River, Huailai County, is the largest best-preserved post station cluster in China. Its most distinctive features are of important historical and artistic value.

鸡鸣驿站城楼

据《镇志·堡城图》记载："隆庆砖修重券东西城门越城越楼各二座。""越城"平面形状类似于故宫午门双阙式门台，城门左右各有较长墙台对称突出墙体之外，夹门而立，城门里面，门台亦突出墙外，东西两门虽无瓮城，但以双阙护门，起到了瓮城作用。

Jiming Post Station Gate Tower

Location: Jiming Post Station

This city gate has long symmetrical terraces extending out beside the gate on both sides, inside as well as outside the city wall. Although there is no barbican on the east and west gates, there are double watchtowers serving to guard the gate.

2010年7月

> 鸡鸣驿站文昌宫

　　文昌宫是供奉文昌帝君的地方，但其自建成起，就成为驿站子弟及城内富家子弟上学的地方，故此宫兼有文庙的作用。文昌宫格局严谨，包括山门、文昌庙、斋堂、七贤祠等，是重要的邮驿附属文物。

Wenchang Temple in Jiming Post Station

Location: Jiming Post Station

Wenchang Hall is a place to worship Wenchang Emperor. However, later, it became a school for children of the Post Station and wealthy family within the town.

2007年9月

鸡鸣驿站城楼一角

驿城城楼造型生动、古朴雄壮。城楼为该驿站的象征标志,东门马道建于门台北侧,长16米,宽近4米,现有38步台阶可供攀登。

View of Jiming Post Station Gate Tower

Location: Jiming Post Station

The Gate Tower is the symbol of the Post Station. East Gate of Horse Avenue, built on the north edge of the terrace, is 16m by wide 4m. 38 steps lead up to it.

2007年5月

| 鸡鸣驿站驿馆 |

　　驿馆位于驿城内西北,是专供过往官员、驿卒就餐住宿的"公馆院"。这座三进院落的北屋,隔扇的木插销头做工考究,各个木插销头分别刻有琴、棋、书、画、莲、蝙蝠、蝉等不同的形象,栩栩如生。

Inn in Jiming Post Station
Location: Jiming Post Station
The Inn located in the northwest of the town and provided food and accommodation for traveling officers and officials.

2007年5月

鸡鸣驿站影壁

精美的影壁体现了中国传统建筑尤其是砖雕建筑的精湛技艺。它们历经风雨，伫立在乡间几百年，守护着一户户古老的宅院。在驿站，有些影壁因年久失修，面临着倒塌的危险，还有些老宅院的影壁因宅院改造翻新而被拆除，让人痛心不已。

Screen Wall of Jiming Post Station

Location: Jiming Post Station

This delicate screen wall reflects the exquisite craftsmanship of traditional Chinese architecture, especially brick carving architecture.

2007年5月

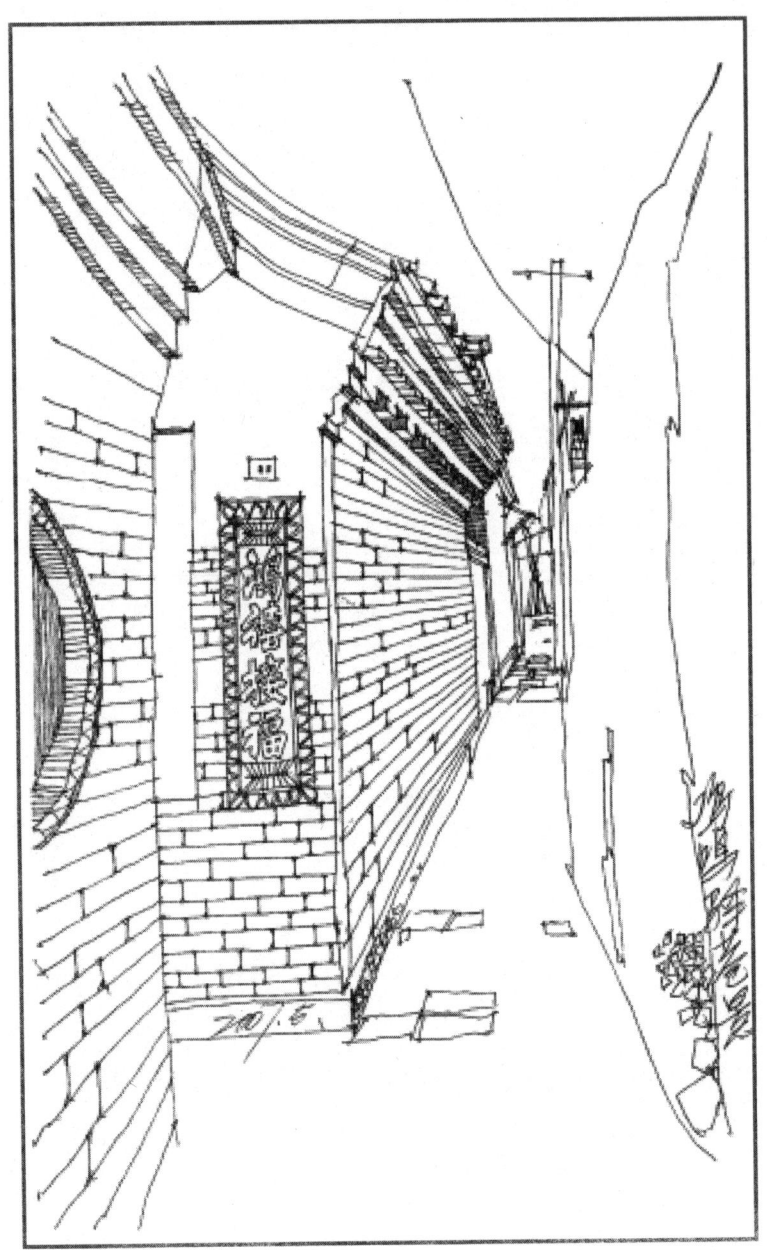

2007年5月

鸡鸣驿站巷景

此巷位于驿站贺家大院以东。八国联军打进北京，慈禧太后和光绪皇帝西逃，在鸡鸣驿站住过一宿，似乎给这一普通的院落带来一个荣耀的故事，后人因此留下"鸿禧接福"的字样。

Lane in Jiming Post Station

Location: Jiming Post Station

The lane is located in the east of He's Courtyard in Post Station. Empress Dowager Cixi and Emperor Guangxu stayed here one night. A tablet placed here inscribed with "Hong Xi Jie Fu" (Receiving Fortune) commemorates the visit.

元中都遗址

元中都遗址位于张家口张北县馒头营乡，始建于元大德十一年（1307），与当时的元大都、元上都齐名。元中都的建造者为元世祖忽必烈的曾孙元武宗海山。元中都遗址的挖掘工作为研究元代都城形制提供了新的实例。

Yuanzhong City Relic

Location: Zhangbei County, Zhangjiakou

Yuanzhong City Relic is located in Mantou Yingxiang, Zhangbei County, Zhangjiakou, which was built in 1307 by Emperor Wuzong of the Yuan Dynasty, the great-grandson of Emperor Kublai Khan, first emperor of Yuan Dynasty.

2011年1月

2011年10月

开阳堡

　　开阳堡是张家口市阳原县浮图讲乡的一个行政村。这里是战国时期的赵国代郡安阳邑，是阳原县境内最古老的村庄。堡内街区为井字结构，史称"九宫街"，目前还保留着"乾三连"和"坤三连"的格局，仍能看到依八卦图建造的痕迹。开阳堡最宝贵的价值，在于保留了千年古城的整体风貌。

Kaiyang Fort

Location: Yangyuan County, Zhangjiakou

Kaiyang Fort is an administrative village of Futu Jiangxiang, Yangyuan County, Zhangjiakou. Streets within the fort are in tic-tac-toe layout, which shows a construction technique according to the Eight Elements Diagram. The most precious value of Kaiyang Fort is the complete preservation of a thousand-year-old ancient city.

南安寺塔

南安寺塔位于蔚县县城中心，始建于北魏，辽、金重修，从塔的造型和风格看，塔基、塔座为清代重修。此塔为八角十三级密檐式实心砖塔，高约28米，用条石叠砌的塔基高2.5米，一至三层为木构出檐，以上为仿木砖檐，一至三层及十三层的角檐有铁套兽，四至十二层为陶套兽。南安寺塔是全国重点文物保护单位。

Nan'an Temple Pagoda

Location: Yuxian County, Zhangjiakou

Nan'an Temple Pagoda, located in the center of Yuxian County, was built during the North Wei Dynasty (386-534). It is a 13-storey octagonal solid brick pagoda, about 28m high with a 2.5m high base built with stone bars. F/1-F/3 has eaves made of wood; eaves on other floors are made of wood-like bricks.

2009年9月

玉皇阁（一）

　　在蔚县城北城垣上有一座庄严壮观、气度不凡的建筑——玉皇阁。玉皇阁始建于明洪武十年（1377），坐北面南，正殿按"明三暗二"的格局建筑，外观三层，实为两层，平面呈长方形，上下阁楼均为面宽五间、进深四间。

Jade Emperor's Palace (1)

Location: Yuxian County, Zhangjiakou

Jade Emperor's Palace built on the city wall in north Yuxian County in 1377 faces the south and has two rectangular shape storeys.

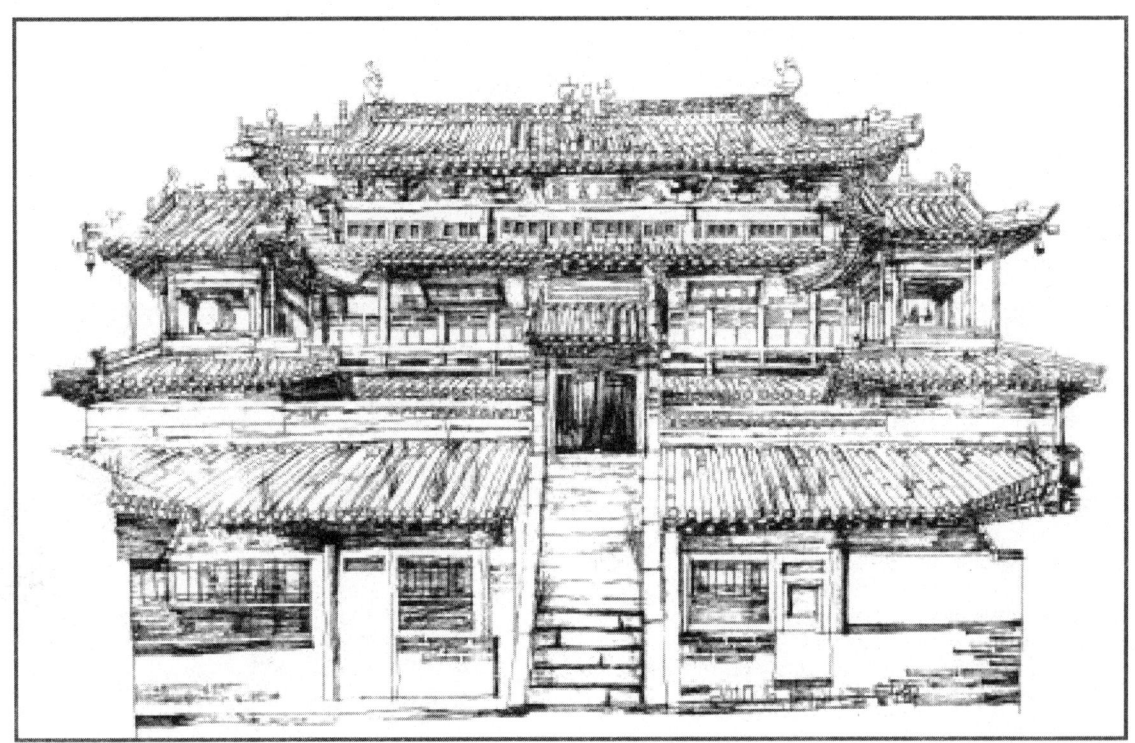

2010年5月

玉皇阁 (二)

玉皇阁作为蔚县"铁城"之一角,与东西南三门之三楼并峙,成为蔚州古城的屏藩,起着瞭望敌情、防御外侮的重要作用。

Jade Emperor's Palace (2)

Location: Yuxian County, Zhangjiakou

As an integral part of Yuxian Tiecheng, Jade Emperor's Palace is opposite to three buildings in three city gates in east, west and south, forming screen for ancient Weizhou to observe enemies and defend invaders.

2007年9月

玉皇阁（三）

玉皇阁历经风雨剥蚀、战乱兵灾，虽几经重建，依然完整地矗立于高高的城垣之上。现存仍为明代建筑风格，表现出中国古代能工巧匠的高超技艺和智慧，是研究明初建筑艺术的重要实例。蔚县玉皇阁是全国重点文物保护单位。

Jade Emperor's Palace (3)

Location: Yuxian County, Zhangjiakou

Enduring wind and rain, wars and disasters, Jade Emperor's Palace still stands intact high on the city wall after several reconstructions. Its architectural style is that of the Ming Dynasty.

2009年9月

| 暖泉书院魁星楼 |

　　暖泉镇位于蔚县之西，以镇中心有一股三冬不冻的泉水而得名，书院亦因之而得名。整个书院以泉为胜，书院东北角筑有魁星楼，为三层砖木式结构，可沿楼梯登上顶层极目远眺。蔚县暖泉镇是全国历史文化名镇。

Kuixing Building in Nuanquan Academy

Location: Yuxian County, Zhangjiakou

Located in west Yuxian County, a hot spring in the center of the town gave it the name "Nuanquan Town". It is also the name of the academy. The spring adds interest to the academy. This view is of Kuixing Building - a three-storey brick and wood structure northeast of the academy.

2007年9月

西古堡北门楼

　　西古堡又称寨堡，位于蔚县暖泉镇之西，始建于明嘉靖年间（1522~1566），重修于清代，为典型的北方村寨围堡。清顺治、康熙年间，为加强防御功能，在该堡南北堡门外又暂筑一座瓮城，因似虎的两只前爪，被百姓誉为"虎抱头"，北瓮城原有九天阁等建筑。

North Gatehouse of Xigubu

Location: Yuxian County, Zhangjiakou

Xigubu, a castle, located in the east of Nuoquan Town, Yuxian County, was built during the reign of Ming Emperor Jiajing (1522-1566). Its typical enclosed stockade village in north China.

2007年9月

【西古堡北门楼一景】

西古堡内的村民安逸友善，在街头巷尾常能看到推着小车叫卖的场景，将古堡点缀得更加纯朴。

View of North Gatehouse, Xigubu

Location: Yuxian County, Zhangjiakou

Villagers of Xigubu are friendly and live a pleasant life. They sell goods on the street from their carts, giving the castle a more rustic air.

2011年3月

2010年6月

西古堡民居门楼（一）

西古堡的民居依然保留着传统的风格，门楼的装饰也原汁原味，虽然有的都歪斜了，可细看，上面的砖雕、木雕都是极其讲究的手艺，细腻程度不在山西民居之下。

Residential Gatehouse of Xigubu (1)

Location: Yuxian County, Zhangjiakou

Residential houses in Xigubu still retain the traditional style, and the gatehouse maintains its authentic decoration. Although some of them have been damaged, the brick and wood carvings are of exquisite craftsmanship.

西古堡民居门楼（二）

古堡的四合院民居，其完整的民居格局、门楣精美的砖雕木雕让人折服。

Residential Gatehouse of Xigubu (2)

Location: Yuxian County, Zhangjiakou

Courtyard houses in the ancient castle preserve the complete residential layout and exquisite brick and wood carvings on the lintel - always astonishing visitors.

2010年6月

2010年10月

源影塔

源影塔位于秦皇岛昌黎县城内西北隅,因塔所在地有一"源影寺"而得名,寺院早已倒毁,唯古塔独存。从塔的建筑风格看,属辽、金时期塔型,为八角十三层实心密檐,高36米。塔的主体为砖木结构,塔基上有须弥座。此塔雄伟壮观,古人称之"霞晖窣睹"。昌黎源影塔是全国重点文物保护单位。

Yuanying Pagoda

Location: Qinhuangdao

A view of Yuanying Pagoda located in the northwest of Changli County, Qinhuangdao. It took its name from "Yuanying Temple" which was destroyed long ago, leaving the ancient pagoda standing alone. It is 13-storey octagonal solid multi-eave pagoda 36m high. Its main body is brick and wood with double lotus petals on the base.

| 山海关城楼一角 |

　　山海关城池与长城相连，以城为关，城高14米，厚7米。全城有四座主要城门，并有防御建筑，是一座防御体系比较完整的城关，有"天下第一关"之称。此城楼耸立于秦皇岛段长城之上，登上城楼二楼，可俯视山海关城全貌及关外的原野。山海关是全国重点文物保护单位。

View of Shanhai Pass City Tower

Location: Qinhuangdao

Shanhai Pass is one of the passes of the Great Wall. The city tower is 14m high and 7m wide. There are four major gatehouses in the city with defensive buildings. This is a city tower with the complete defensive system, winning it the honor of "first pass of the world".

2010年6月

清东陵

清东陵位于唐山遵化市马兰峪西,是我国现存规模庞大、体系完整的帝王陵墓群之一。共建有皇陵五座:顺治帝的孝陵、康熙帝的景陵、乾隆帝的裕陵、咸丰帝的定陵、同治帝的惠陵,以及后陵四座、妃园五座、公主陵一座。

Qingdong Mausoleum

Location: Tangshan

Qingdong Mausoleum, located in Malan Valley east of Zunhua, Tangshan, is one of the grand and better preserved imperial mausoleums in China. There are five imperial mausoleums: Xiaoling of Emperor Shunzhi, Jingling Mausoleum of Emperor Kangxi, Yuling Mausoleum of Emperor Qianlong, Dingling of Emperor Xianfeng, and Huiling Mausoleum of Emperor Tongzhi. There are 4 empress mausoleums, 5 imperial concubine gardens and 1 princess mausoleum.

2009年8月

孝东陵方城明楼

孝东陵位于孝陵东侧，内葬顺治皇帝的孝惠章皇后以及二十八名妃子、格格、福晋。建于清康熙五十七年（1718），方城明楼是陵中最高的建筑物。

Xiaodong Mausoleum Fangcheng Ming Building

Location: Tangshan

Xiaodong Mausoleum, located to the east of Xiaoling, is the burial site of Xiaohui Zhang Empress and 28 imperial concubines, princesses, and wives of princes. It was built in 1718. Fangcheng Ming Building is the tallest in the mausoleum.

2009年7月

景陵一角

　　景陵是康熙皇帝的陵寝,是清朝在东陵界内营建的第二座皇帝陵,建筑规模总体上是以孝陵为蓝本,但局部又有所改创。景陵石像生的布置有别于清代所有帝陵,自五孔桥至牌楼门段的神路由于地形的影响而呈弯环的曲线,呈现出灵活多变的特点。

View of Jingling Mausoleum

Location: Tangshan

Jingling Mausoleum, the tomb of Emperor Kangxi, was the second imperial mausoleum built within Dongling during the Qing Dynasty. Ranging in a ring-shape curve from Five-arch Bridge to God Road in Archway Gate due to the land form, the stone sculptures and stone beasts in Jingling Mausoleum are different from all other imperial mausoleums of the Qing Dynasty, because of their varied layout.

2010年10月

> 裕陵

  裕陵是乾隆皇帝的陵寝,位于孝陵以西的胜水峪,始建于乾隆八年(1743),乾隆十七年(1752)告竣。裕陵明堂开阔、建筑崇宏、工精料美、气势非凡,其规制既承袭了前朝,又有所创新。

Yuling Mausoleum

Location: Tangshan

Yuling Mausoleum, the tomb of Emperor Qianlong, is located in Shengshui Valley east of Xiaoling. Construction began in 1743 and was completed in 1752.

2011年6月

> 惠陵

　　惠陵是同治皇帝的陵寝，位于景陵东南3公里处的双山峪。同治帝死后，1875年春，清廷选择双山峪为万年吉地，确定陵名为惠陵，惠陵建筑规制依照定陵。

Huiling Mausoleum

Location: Tangshan

Huiling Mausoleum, the tomb of Emperor Tongzhi, is located in Shuangshan Valley 3km to the southeast of Jingling Mausoleum. In the spring of 1875 after Emperor Tongzhi died. The Qing government regarded Shuangshan Valley as an auspicious place and named the mausoleum Huiling Mausoleum.

2010年7月

唐山玉田净觉寺牌楼

　　净觉寺位于玉田县杨家套乡蛮子营村东,坐落在还乡河畔。其始建于唐代,历经宋、金、辽、元、明、清修建,净觉寺主体建筑有三殿、三楼,展现在今人面前的仍保留了它宽敞、豁达、庄严和肃穆的风貌。净觉寺是全国重点文物保护单位。

Tangshan Yutian Jingjue Temple Archway

Location:Tangshan

Jingjue Temple is located in the east of Manziying Village, Yangjiatao Town, Yutian County, beside the Huanxiang River. It was first built during the Tang Dynasty (618-907), and repeatedly repaired during later dynasties: Song, Jin, Liao, Yuan, Ming and Qing. The main building of Jingjue Temple has three halls and three towers. It still retains its spacious, open, solemn and respectful style. Jingjue Temple is a national key cultural relic protection unit.

2007年6月

2008年6月

大旗杆

保定直隶总督署门前，原有两个木质旗杆，高约20米，上刷红漆，是署衙的标志。1920年，直鲁豫巡阅使曹锟在原来的位置重建钢筋混凝土旗杆。大旗杆由底座、旗杆、旗斗三部分组成，旗斗为方形。

Great Flagpole

Location: Baoding

In front of the Governor's Office of Zhili Province Baoding, there were two red-painted wooded flagpoles 20m high which were the symbol of the Yamen. In 1920, the governor of Zhili, Shandong and Henan provinces told Cao Kun to build reinforced concrete flagpoles to replace the original wooden ones.

> 保定大悲阁

据《保定府志》载，宋淳祐十年（1250），蒙古河北东西路都元帅张柔修建大悲阁。现在的大悲阁是清代乾隆年间被焚后多次重修的建筑。

Baoding Dabei Pavilion

Location: Baoding

According to *The Baoding Annals*, Zhang Rou, General of East and West City of North of Mongolia River, built Dabei Pavilion in 1250. The Pavilion we see today was destroyed by fire four times and rebuilt during the reign of Qing Emperor Qianlong (1736-1795).

2012年2月

保定古莲池

保定古莲池前身为金哀宗正大四年（1227）张柔所营建的雪香园，是中国北方现存最古的园林之一，清雍正十一年（1733）又于此地开莲池书院。古莲池位于保定市中心，在技法上讲求生机、含蓄、深远、协调，呈天然之趣。保定古莲池是全国重点文物保护单位。

Baoding Ancient Lotus Pond

Location: Baoding

Located in the center of Baoding, the predecessor of Boading Ancient Lotus Pond was Snow-Fragrance Garden built by Zhang Rou in 1227 and is one of the most ancient gardens preserved in north China. In 1733, Lotus Pond Academy was built here.

2008年6月

【碑刻长廊】

古莲池北端的碑刻长廊长达33米，嵌有82方碑刻，游人可在此欣赏书法瑰宝。

Tablet Gallery

Location: Ancient Lotus Pond

The Tablet Gallery on the north edge of Ancient Lotus Pond is 33m long. There are 82 carved tablets on display here. Visitors can appreciate the calligraphy treasures here.

2008年6月

水东楼

莲池自古就环水置景，池旁水东楼是一座二层小楼，小巧玲珑，优雅别致，拙中见巧，朴中有奇，登楼可览园中全景。

Shuidong Building

Location: Ancient Lotus Pond

The lotus pond has had special landscapes set up along its banks since ancient times. One of these, Shuidong Building is a small 2-storey, graceful, and picturesque structure. From its upper floor, the entire garden can be seen.

2012年1月

藻咏楼

藻咏楼位于古莲池中心位置,为马鞍形双重檐脊,底层红柱明廊,栏槛环绕,楼堂上下棱窗锦幔。

Zaoyong Building

Location: Ancient Lotus Pond

Zaoyong Building, located in the center of Ancient Lotus Pond, has a saddle-shaped double-eave ridge roof and a bright red pillared corridor with a surrounding fence below.

2008年6月

2010年1月

直隶图书馆

直隶图书馆即原河北省图书馆，位于古莲池院内，为一座两层西式楼房。1908年，直隶省提学使卢靖筹款，在古莲池东部建立直隶图书馆，收藏图书两千余种，是当时长江以北地区最早建立的公共图书馆，至今服务社会已超过百年。

Zhili Library
Location: Ancient Lotus Pond
Zhili Library, the former Hebei Library, is located within a courtyard of Ancient Lotus Pond, is 2-storey western-style building. It has served society for over 100 years.

保定光园正门

光园位于保定市区裕华路中段，原为明代大宁都司右卫署和断事司。清康熙二年（1663），直隶巡抚由正定迁到保定后，巡道司狱署驻此。雍正二年（1724）又改为按察使司狱署。1916年，曹锟任直隶督军时，在光园大兴土木，进行大规模改建、装饰，此处成为曹锟的公馆。因曹锟非常敬慕抗倭名将戚继光，故将此处改名为光园。光园正门为砖石结构的拱形券门，券门上有突出两侧墙高的仿西洋装饰。

Gate of Baoding Guangyuan Garden

Location: Baoding

Guangyuan Garden, located in the middle of Yuhua Road, Baoding downtown, was formerly a prison office of the Ming Dynasty (1368-1644). In 1916, it was converted into Cao Kun's mansion when he was military governor of Zhili Province. The gate of Guangyuan Park was a brick and stone arched gate; atop the two side walls were Western decorations.

2007年9月

定州考棚

定州考棚也叫贡院，位于定州市中山东路草场胡同，始建于清乾隆三年（1738），曾于道光十三年（1833）重修，是北方地区唯一保存下来的中国古代科举考试的场所。定州考棚是全国重点文物保护单位。

Dingzhou Examination Hall

Location: Dingzhou, Baoding

Dingzhou Examination Hall, also known as Examination Hall, is located in Caochang Hutong, Zhongshan East Road, Dingzhou. It was initially built in 1738 and rebuilt in 1833. It is the only examination venue of feudal China preserved in the north.

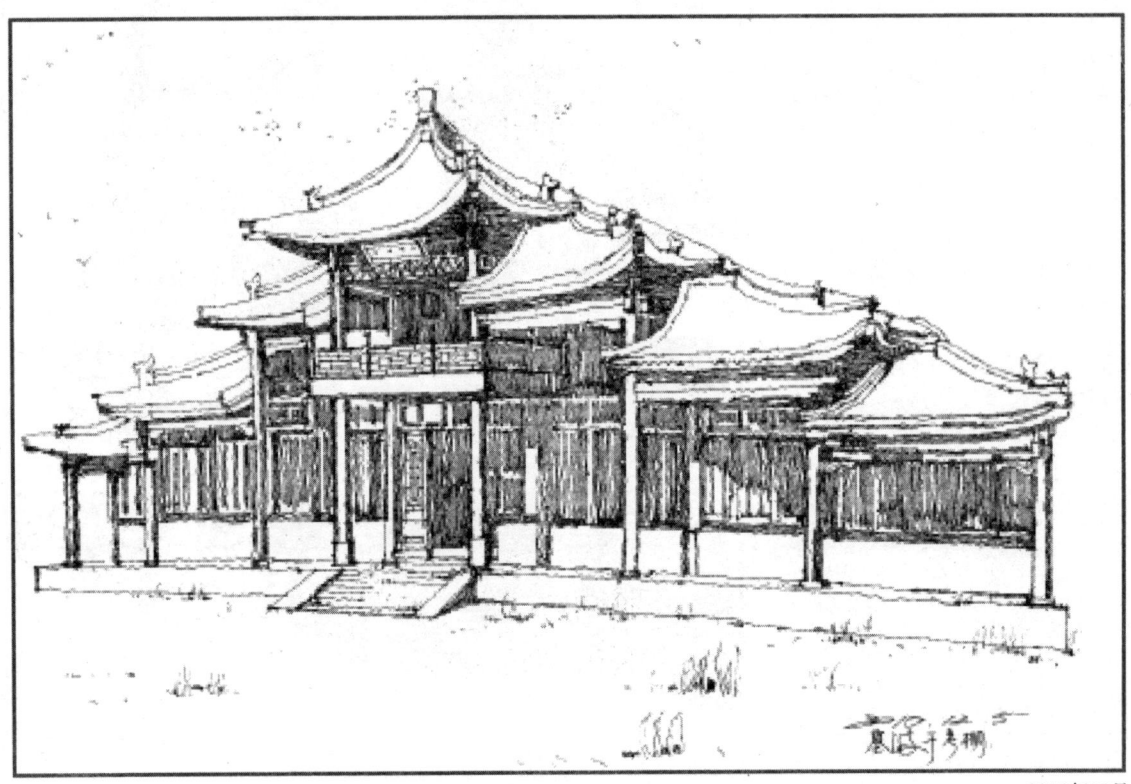

2010年12月

> 保定西大街

　　保定西大街是以商业建筑为主的兼有衙署、学府、祠堂、金融、民居建筑的一条历史文化街区，现存清初及以前建筑两个、民国期间建筑九个，中西合璧，整体上是清末民初的建筑风格。一般是坡顶、灰墙、半圆拱顶门窗、立面有装饰线和花饰，以砖雕成，做工精细。

Baoding Xida Street

Location: Baoding

Baoding Xida Street was a historical and cultural street with important commercial buildings as well as governmental buildings, schools, shrines, financial institutions, and residential buildings in Western and Chinese styles. The entire street has maintained architectural style of the late Qing Dynasty and early Republican Periods.

2008年5月

腰山王氏庄园

　　王氏庄园始建于清代初年，位于保定市顺平县腰山镇，主要建筑布局成四方形，坐北朝南。整座建筑以灰色调为主，古朴大方，给人以庄重典雅的感觉。腰山王氏庄园是中国古代建筑史上一处罕见的超规制清代城堡式民居建筑群，是全国重点文物保护单位。

Wang's Manor in Yaoshan
Location: Shunping County, Baoding

Wang's Manor was built during the early Qing Dynasty (1644-1911) in Yaoshan Town, Shunping County, Baoding. It is a grey, square structure facing south. It is a rare large Qing-style castle-like residential building of ancient Chinese architecture.

2009年6月

北岳庙德宁殿

北岳庙位于保定曲阳县城内西南部，主殿德宁殿重建于元世祖至元七年（1270），为我国现存元代木结构建筑中最大的一座。德宁殿建于高台上，四周以走廊环绕，重檐大顶，外观雄伟。德宁殿是全国重点文物保护单位。

Beiyue Temple Dening Hall

Location: Quyang County, Baoding

Beiyue Temple is located in southwest Quyang County, Baoding. The main hall - Dening Hall, rebuilt in 1270, is the largest extant wooded structure of the Yuan Dynasty (1271-1368) in China.

2010年6月

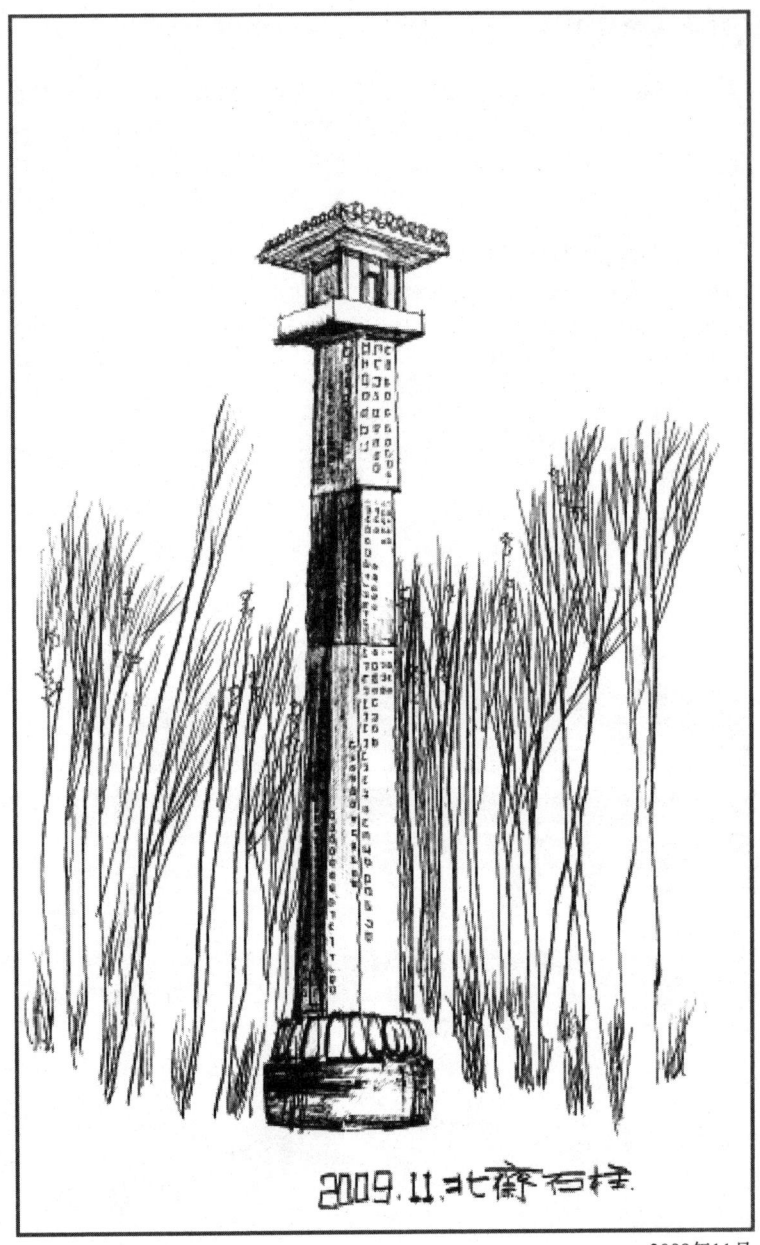

2009年11月

北齐石柱

北齐石柱位于保定城北60公里处定兴县县城西北石柱村，建于北齐天统五年（569），是南北朝遗存至今的少数建筑之一。全柱分基础、柱身和石屋三部分，通高6.65米，设计精美、雕刻细腻、造型奇特。刻在石柱各面的《标异乡义慈惠石柱颂》具有重要的史料价值。此文共3400余字，记叙了自北魏孝昌元年至永安元年间的一次大规模的农民起义。此石柱是全国重点文物保护单位。

Beiqi Stone Column

Location: Dingxing County, Baoding

Beiqi Stone Column is located in Shizhu Village, northwest to Dingxing County, 60km north to Baoding. It was built in 569. The "Ode of Charity of Foreign Villages" engraved on each side of the column is of significant historical value.

保定安国药王庙

药王庙坐落于安国市城南，始建于北宋太平兴国年间（976-984），经明、清历次修葺成为现在的规模。药王庙山门外的牌坊为重檐庑殿式建筑，由黄色琉璃瓦覆盖，三间四柱，彩饰斗拱。牌坊两侧铁铸旗杆上的风铃给人一种悠远肃穆的感觉。

Baoding An'guo Yaowang Temple

Location: Baoding

Yaowang Temple is located in the south of An'guo city. It was first built during the Northern Song Dynasty, Xingguo Period (976-984) and repaired several times during the Ming and Qing dynasties. Later, it took on today's form and scale. Outside the gate of Yaowang Temple is the memorial archway, a double-eave hip roof building. Four columns in three bays are covered by yellow glazed tiles, with colorful Dougong architectural features. The sonorous wind bell hanging the cast iron flagpoles on the both sides of the memorial archway exudes a kind of distant solemn and respectful feeling.

2006年9月

隆兴寺

隆兴寺位于石家庄正定县城东门里街,是国内保存时代较早、规模较大而又保存完整的佛教寺院之一。始建于隋代,时称"龙藏寺",唐代时改名为"龙兴寺",至宋代时落成为规模宏大的建筑群,之后历经多次修葺,直至清代康熙年间,形成了东、中、西三路并举的建筑格局,规制日益完善,达到鼎盛。

Longxing Temple

Location: Zhengding County, Shijiazhuang

Longxing Temple located within East Gate of Zhengding County, Shijiazhuang, is one of the best preserved, earlier large Buddhist temples in China. It was initially built during the Sui Dynasty (518-618) and repaired many time. Its most prosperous period was the reign of Qing Emperor Kangxi (1662-1722).

摩尼殿

摩尼殿坐落于隆兴寺内,建于宋仁宗皇祐四年(1052),面阔七间,进深七间,殿平面近正方形,四面各出抱厦一座,外观为重檐九脊殿,四面抱厦各以山面向前。

Moni Hall

Location: Longxing Temple

Moni Hall, a square structure, was built in 1052 within Longxing Temple.

2010年8月

大悲阁

大悲阁是隆兴寺中轴线的主体建筑，始建于宋，后毁于兵。清末重建为三层五檐歇山之大阁，并设平座，高峻挺拔，又名佛香阁。

Dabei Pavilion

Location: Longxing Temple

Dabei Pavilion, the main structure in central axis of Longxing Temple, was initially built during the Song Dynasty (960-1279), but ruined by war, was rebuilt during the late Qing Dynasty (1616-1911).

2012年2月

转轮藏阁

转轮藏阁位于大悲阁前西侧，与东侧的慈氏阁相对而立。阁坐西朝东，面阔三间，进深四间，重檐歇山顶，平面近似方形。

Zhuanlun Collection Pavilion

Location: Longxing Temple

Zhuanlun Collection Pavilion at the west in the front of Dabei Pavilion, is opposite Cishi Pavilion to the east.

2010年8月

2008年3月

转轮藏

转轮藏为八角形旋转书架，中有立轴，为旋转之中心。其经屉以上，做成重檐状，下檐八角，其上不用椽，仅用雁翅板，上施山华蕉叶。

Zhuanlun Repository
Location: Longxing Temple
Zhuanlun Repository is an octagonal bookshelf rotating on a vertical shaft.

隆兴寺外

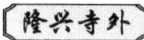

隆兴寺外清幽宁静。

Longxing Temple Setting

Location: Longxing Temple

The setting of Longxing Temple is tranquil and beautiful.

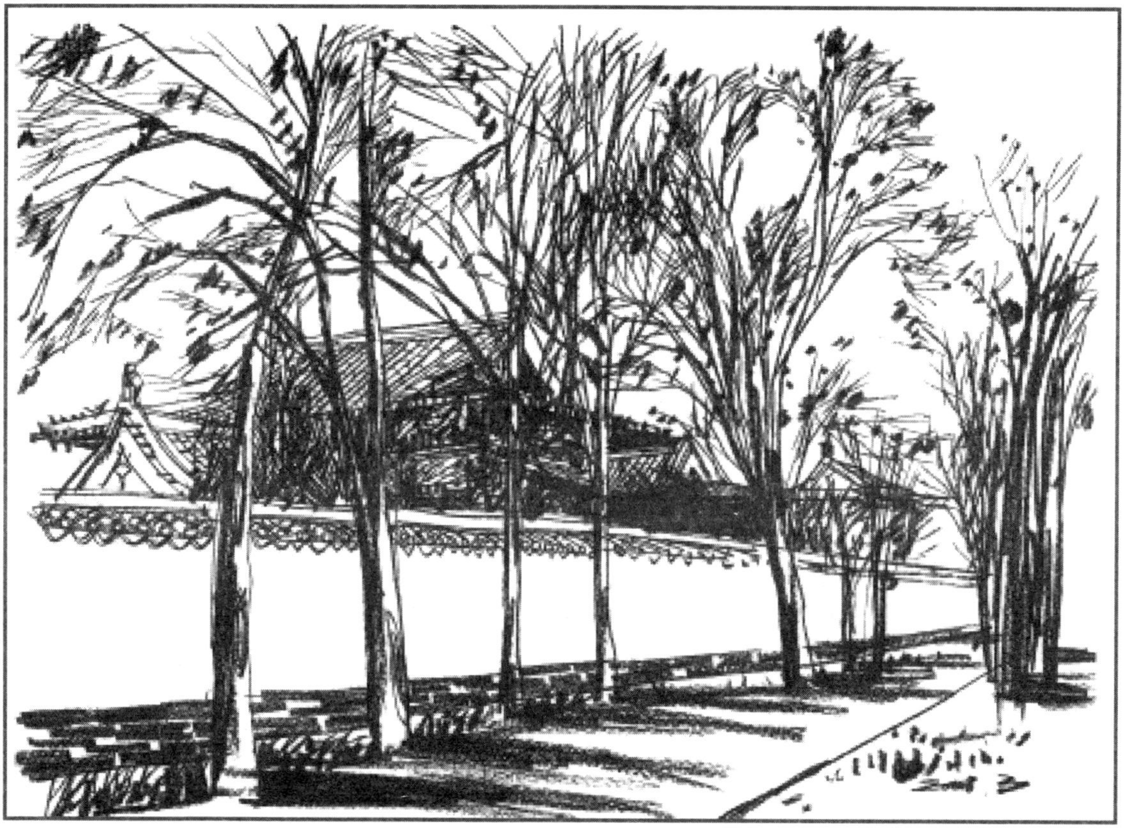

2008年3月

2005年11月

开元寺塔

开元寺塔又称雁塔，坐落于石家庄正定县正定钟楼西侧，根据现存实物并结合历史记载推断，此塔可能始建于唐贞观十年（636），唐乾宁五年（898）重建，后虽经历代修葺但依然保持唐代建筑特点，是我国建筑宝库的珍贵遗产。开元寺塔是全国重点文物保护单位。

Kaiyuan Temple Pagoda

Location: Zhengding County, Shijiazhuang

Kaiyuan Temple Pagoda, also known as Wild Goose Pagoda, is located at the west side of Zhengding Clock Tower of Zhengding County, Shijiazhuang. Inferred from the existing physical evidence as well as historical records, this tower was probably built in 636. Though it was repaired time after time during past dynasties, its architectural features of the Tang Dynasty (618-907) remain unchanged.

正定广惠寺华塔

广惠寺花塔位于正定县县城南隅民生街广惠寺内，广惠寺已殿宇无存，仅余孤塔。塔始建于唐代前期，后历代均有重修，至金皇统年间（1141-1149）被毁，20年后即金大定年间（1161-1189）才得重新修复，所以，现存之花塔当为金代大定年间重修后遗物。广惠寺华塔是全国重点文物保护单位。

Zhengding Huata Pagoda of Guanghui Temple

Location: Shijiazhuang

Huata Pagoda of the Guanghui Temple is located in Minsheng Street in the South of Zhengding County. Today, no halls of Guanghui Temple remain, only the pagoda is left. The pagoda was first built in the early Tang Dynasty (618-907) and repaired during later dynasties. During the Jin Dynasty Huang Tong Period(1141-1149), the pagoda was destroyed. After twenty years, during the Jin Dynasty Dading Period (1161-1189), it was fully rebuilt. Today's Hua Pagoda is the legacy of the Jin Dynasty Dading Period, and is a national key cultural relic protection unit.

2008年9月

| 赵州桥 |

　　始建于隋代的赵州石桥位于石家庄赵县城南的洨河上，全长64米，主拱跨径37米，拱券矢高7米有余，拱顶宽9米。整体结构采取纵向并列砌筑法，用三道相对独立的拱券并排组成桥拱主体。赵州桥是全国重点文物保护单位，具有极高的历史文化价值。

Zhaozhou Bridge

Location: Zhaoxian County, Shijiazhuang

Zhaozhou Bridge, a stone-arched bridge located on the Xiaohe River in the southern part of Zhaoxian County, Shijiazhuang, was built in the Sui Dynasty with a length of 64m and a main arch span of 37m. The overall structure of the bridge is a longitudinal and parallel masonry. Three comparatively independent arches were arranged side-by-side to form the main arch of the bridge.

2005年11月

赵州桥栏板

自20世纪50年代赵州桥大修以来，桥上雕刻精美的石制栏板被移至室内陈列，石桥装饰细部多以仿品替换。

Stone Fascia Panels of Zhaozhou Bridge

Location: Zhaozhou Bridge

The delicately carved stone fascia panels were brought to the indoor display rooms after Zhaozhou Bridge was remodeled in the 1950s. They were replaced by imitations.

2000年10月

2010年5月

陀罗尼经幢

陀罗尼经幢位于石家庄赵县县城内南大街与石塔路相交的十字路口处，建于北宋宝元元年（1038），通体石造，高15米余，幢身为八角形，由下往上经幢逐渐收小。现存宋代诸幢中，赵县陀罗尼经幢体量最大，且形象华丽、雕刻精美。此经幢是全国重点文物保护单位。

Dharani Sutra Pillar

Location: Zhaoxian County, Shijiazhuang

Dharani Sutra Pillar is located at the intersection of South Street and Shita Road in Zhaoxian County, Shijiazhuang. Built in 1038, it was made of stone with a height of 15m. The octagonal pillar gradually decreases in diameter from bottom to top.

赵州禅师舍利塔

赵州禅师舍利塔建于元天历三年（1330），为密檐式砖木结构，平面呈八角形，共七级，是我国古塔中的杰出作品。它精巧优美、高耸巍峨、气势雄伟，为晚唐时禅宗巨匠赵州禅师的舍利塔。此塔是全国重点文物保护单位。

Stupa of Buddhist Monk Zhaozhou

Location: Zhaoxian County, Shijiazhuang

The Stupa of Buddhist Monk Zhaozhou was built in 1330. It is made of brick and wood with highly decorated ledges. The octagon, seven-storey, pagoda is one of the most outstanding works of ancient pagodas in China. It's the Stupa of the Great Buddhist Monk Zhaozhou of the late Tang Dynasty (618- 907).

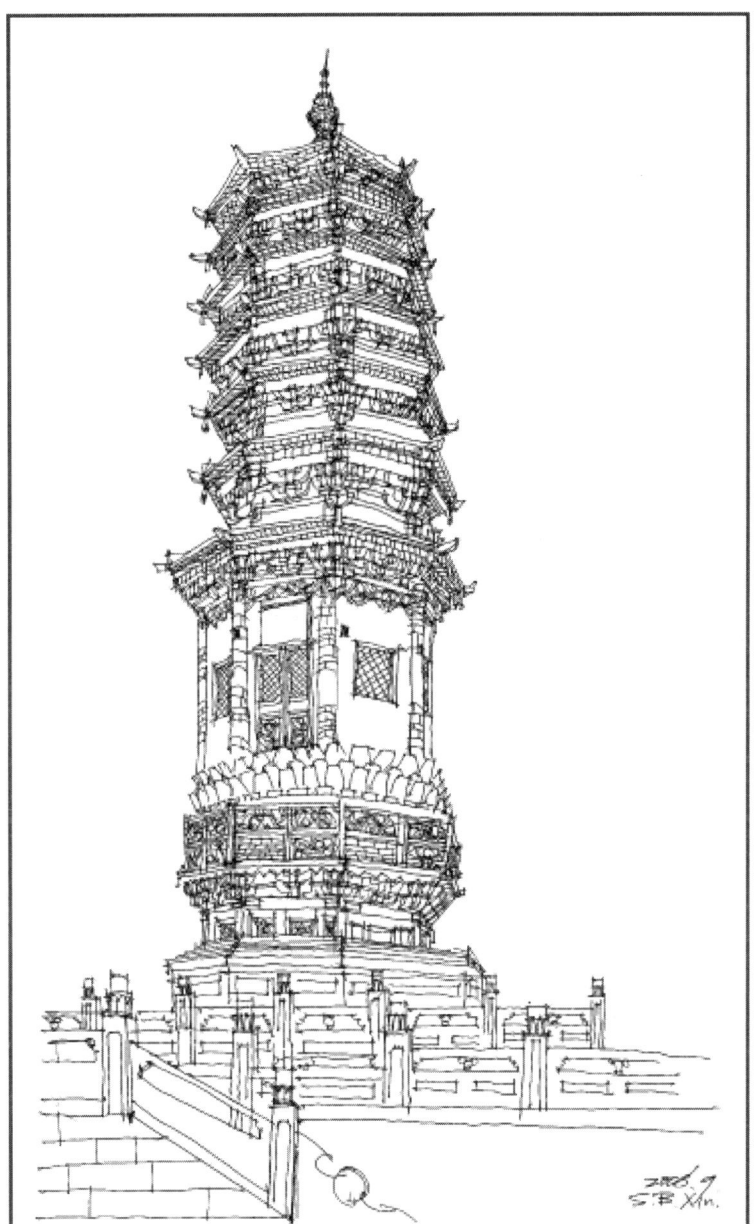

2006年9月

井陉县天长镇城隍庙

据资料记载，井陉县天长镇始建于宋代，城隍庙始建于明代。据清光绪《井陉县志》载，城隍庙在县治西，道光二十三年（1843），邑中绅民捐资重修。城隍庙建在较平缓地带，中轴线上分布着山门、戏楼、大殿及东西配殿。天长镇是全国历史文化名镇。

Town God Temple of Tianchang, Jingxing County

Location: Jingxing County, Shijiazhuang

According to historical records, Tianchang, Jingxing County was built during the Song Dynasty (960-1279) and the Town God Temple during the Ming Dynasty (1368-1644). The Temple was built in a relatively flat area; Along the north-south central axis are the gate, the opera stage, and the main hall; the side halls are along the east and west.

2011年12月

城隍庙戏楼

戏楼位于城隍庙中部，为单檐歇山卷棚亭阁式建筑，形制特别。在歇山顶正中建一四角亭，面阔三间，进深三间。斗拱只有一朵，较简单，仅施单件龙头花拱，在角梁下施一象头状支垫。砖砌台基高大，边用青角石压檐。

Opera Stage of Town God Temple

Location: Jingxing County, Shijiazhuang

The playhouse is located in the middle of Town God Temple. Its pavilion-style architecture with single-eave gable and parabolic roof, is unique.

2011年5月

福庆寺桥楼殿

福庆寺位于井陉县南40公里的苍岩山内。巍峨独特的桥楼殿殿堂建于重山叠翠、峡谷一线处,形成"桥殿飞虹"的天下奇观。桥楼殿为敞肩拱式,翼角高翘,流苏彩绘,高架于云天雾海之上,有高不可攀之威、腾空欲飞之势。桥楼殿是全国重点文物保护单位。

Bridge House Palace of Fuqing Temple

Location: Jingxing County, Shijiazhuang

Fuqing Temple is located on Cangyan Mountain, 40 km south of Jingxing County. The unique towering Bridge House Palace was built across canyons, among the green mountain peaks, forming a wonder of a "bridge house, flying rainbow".

2009年6月

宝云寺塔

宝云寺塔位于衡水市旧城村，为砖木结构，高35米，底座周长25米。张驭寰等先生认为根据一、二层塔檐"批竹头"、"方形圆开"的券门等建造形式看，属唐代建筑风格，而三层以上的座、檐及雕刻的窗棂等又是明显的宋代建筑特点，所以鉴定此塔为北宋初期所建。宝云寺塔是全国重点文物保护单位。

Baoyun Temple Pagoda
Location: Hengshui

Baoyun Temple Posada is located at Old Town Village of Hengshui City. It was made of wood and bricks; it is 35m high and has a 25m perimeter base.

2007年4月

2009年9月

> 邢台县英谈村

英谈村位于邢台县路罗镇,离邢台市区近70公里,距今已有600余年历史。村内有67处院落,依山就势,高低错落,是河北省目前发现的保存最为完好的石寨。整座石寨由红色的山石建筑,仿佛一个红色的城堡。

Yingtan Village, Xingtai County

Location: Xingtai

Yingtan Village is located in Luluo, Xingtai County, about 70 km from downtown Xingtai City. It dates back 600 years ago. With 67 courtyards of varied height in graceful disorder, it is the best preserved stone village in Hebei Province.

英谈村一景

此村具有典型的太行建筑风格，建筑多为明清遗存，错落有致。该村民风纯朴，鸡犬之声相闻。

View of Yingtan Village

Location: Xingtai

This village has a typical Taihang architectural style. Most of the structures are relics of the Ming (1368-1644) and Qing (1644-1911) Dynasties, distributed in picturesque disorder.

2007年5月

响堂山石窟

响堂山石窟位于邯郸峰峰矿区鼓山，分南北两处，相距约15公里。因石窟群在山腰，人们谈笑、拂袖、走动均能发出铿锵的回声，故名响堂山石窟。现存石窟16座，摩崖造像450余龛，大小造像5000余尊，最初开凿于北齐（550~577），以后隋、唐、宋、元、明各代均有增凿。响堂山石窟主要代表了北齐的佛教造像艺术，是短暂的北齐王朝留下的最大的艺术宝库。

Xiangtangshan Grottoes

Location: Handan

Xiangtangshan Grottoes are located at Gushan, Fengfeng Mine, Handan. They are formed by two sections at the north and south at a distance of about 15km. The caves are scattered in the mountainside where sonorous echoes are made when people talk, chuckle or wander inside; this is why it was named Xiangtangshan Grottoes. There are 16 caves, 450 cliff figures and more than 5,000 statues of various sizes here. As a major representative of Buddhist statue art of the Northern Qi Dynasty (550-577), Xiangtangshan Grottoes complex is the largest treasure house of the short-lived Northern Qi Dynasty.

2008年6月

涉县娲皇阁

娲皇宫位于涉县城西的凤凰山上，是我国现存最大、最早的奉祀上古天神女娲氏的古代建筑，是北齐文宣帝高洋往返邺城至晋阳的离宫之一。娲皇宫初开三石室，雕数尊神像，后经历代修葺、续建，分山上山下两组建筑。涉县娲皇宫是全国重点文物保护单位。

娲皇阁坐东面西，为娲皇宫主体建筑，高达23米，为歇山斗拱琉璃瓦顶，悬空而立，构思奇巧，为建筑史上动静结合的杰作。纵观娲皇阁，嵌于绝壁，雕梁画栋，登楼远眺，太行群山涌翠，漳水如带，堪称"天造地设之境"。

Nüwa Goddess Pavilion, She County

Location: Shexian County, Handan

The Palace of Nüwa Goddess is located on Phoenix Mountain in the western part of She County. It is the largest and earliest existing ancient architecture dedicated to the ancient goddess Nüwa. Located at the north and facing the south, and 23m high, Nüwa Goddess Pavilion is the main structure of the Palace.

2010年6月